Thich Nhat Hanh is a world-renowned writer, poet, scholar and Zen Buddhist monk, who lives mostly in the monastic community he founded in France. The author of the *New York Times* bestseller *Anger* and the classic work *The Miracle of Mindfulness*, as well as numerous other books, he conducts public workshops and peace-making retreats throughout the world. He was nominated for the Nobel Peace Prize in 1967.

www.plumvillage.org

By the same author

THICH NHAT HANH

HOW TO
RELAX

'THE FATHER OF MINDFULNESS'
IRISH TIMES

LONDON • SYDNEY • AUCKLAND • JOHANNESBURG

11

Rider, an imprint of Ebury Publishing,
20 Vauxhall Bridge Road,
London SW1V 2SA

Rider is part of the Penguin Random House group
of companies whose addresses can be found at
global.penguinrandomhouse.com

Penguin
Random House
UK

First published in Britain by Rider in 2016
Published in the United States by Parallax Press in 2015

www.penguin.co.uk

Illustrations by Jason DeAntonis

A CIP catalogue record for this book is
available from the British Library

ISBN 9781846045189

Printed and bound in Great Britain by Clays LTD,
Elcograf S.p.A.

CONTENTS

You don't need to set aside special time for resting and relaxing. You don't need a special pillow or any fancy equipment. You don't need a whole hour. In fact, now is a very good time to relax.

You are probably breathing in and out right this moment. If you can close your eyes for a moment, do so. This will help you pay attention to your breath. Your body is doing so many things right now. Your heart is beating. Your lungs are inhaling and exhaling air. Blood is traveling through your veins. Without effort, your body is both working and relaxed.

NOTES
ON RELAXING

RESTING

Whenever animals in the forest are wounded, they rest. They look for a very quiet place and just stay there without moving for many days. They know it's the best way for their body to heal. During this time they may not even eat or drink. The wisdom of stopping and healing is still alive in animals, but we human beings have lost the capacity to rest.

HEALING

We human beings have lost confidence in the body just knowing what to do. If we have time alone with ourselves, we panic and try to do many different things. Mindful breathing helps us to relearn the art of resting. Mindful breathing is like a loving parent cradling a baby, saying, "Don't worry, I'll take good care of you; just rest."

AWARENESS OF BREATHING

Your breathing is a stable, solid ground where you can take refuge. No matter what thoughts, emotions, and perceptions are going on inside you, your breath is always there, like a faithful friend. Whenever you're carried away by thinking, overwhelmed by strong emotions, or feeling restless and dispersed, return to your breathing. Bring body and mind together and anchor your mind. Become aware of the air coming in and going out of your body. With awareness of the breath, our breathing naturally becomes light, calm, and peaceful. At any time of the day or night, whether you're walking, driving, working in the garden, or sitting at the computer, you can return to the peaceful refuge of your own breath.

RESTING POEM

At any moment, we can say this small
poem to ourselves and take a mini-rest.
This poem is like a tiny vacation, except
that it brings you back to your true home
instead of taking you away from it.

> Breathing in, I know I am breathing in.
> Breathing out, I know I am breathing out.

You can even shorten this poem; it works
just as well:

> In.
> Out.

FOLLOWING THE BREATH

To increase your mindfulness and concentration, gently and easily follow your in-breath and out-breath all the way through. Just sitting and following your breathing can bring a lot of joy and healing.

Breathing in, I follow my in-breath all the way through.
Breathing out, I follow my out-breath all the way through.

CALM WATER

Each of us is like the waves and also like
the water. Sometimes we're excited, noisy,
and agitated like the waves. Sometimes
we're tranquil like still water. When water
is calm, it reflects the blue sky, the clouds,
and the trees. Sometimes, whether we're
at home, work, or school, we become
tired, agitated, or unhappy and we need to
transform into calm water. We already have
calmness in us; we just need to know how
to make it manifest.

MEDITATION

To meditate means to pay full attention to something. It doesn't mean to run away from life. Instead it's an opportunity to look deeply into ourselves and into the situation we're in.

STOPPING: THE FIRST ASPECT OF MEDITATION

Meditation has two aspects. The first is stopping (*shamatha* in Sanskrit). We run throughout our whole life, chasing after some idea of happiness. Stopping means to stop our running, our forgetfulness, and our being caught in the past or the future. We come home to the present moment where life is available. The present moment contains every moment. Here we can touch our ancestors, our children, and their children, even if they haven't been born yet. We calm our body and emotions through the practice of mindful breathing, mindful walking, and mindful sitting. Shamatha is also the practice of concentrating, so we can live deeply each moment of our life and touch the deepest level of our being.

STOP FIRST

If we can't rest, it's because we haven't stopped running. We began running a long time ago. We continue to run, even in our sleep. We think that happiness and well-being aren't possible in the present. If you can stop and establish yourself in the here and the now, you will see that there are many elements of happiness available in this moment, more than enough for you to be happy. Even if there are a few things in the present that you dislike, there are still plenty of positive conditions for your happiness. When you walk in the garden, you may see that a tree is dying and so you feel sad and aren't able to enjoy the rest of the garden that is still beautiful. If you look again, you can see that the garden is still beautiful, and you can enjoy it.

LOOKING DEEPLY: THE SECOND ASPECT OF MEDITATION

The second aspect of meditation is looking deeply (*vipashyana* in Sanskrit) in order to see the true nature of things. Understanding is a great gift. Your daily life conducted in mindfulness is also a great gift; this too is the practice of meditation. Mindfulness carries within it concentration and understanding.

MINDFULNESS IN DAILY LIFE

Mindfulness is the continuous practice of touching deeply every moment of daily life. To be mindful is to be truly present with your body and your mind, to harmonize your intentions and actions, and to be in harmony with those around you. We don't need to make a separate time for this outside of our daily activities. We can practice mindfulness in every moment of the day—in the kitchen, the bathroom, or the garden, and as we go from one place to another. We can do the same things we always do—walking, sitting, working, eating, and so on—with mindful awareness of what we're doing. Our mind is with our actions.

A RELAXED POSITION

What is your most relaxed position?
Sometimes we think we can only relax if
we are lying down. But we can also sit in
a relaxed position. Your posture can be
upright and not rigid. Relax your shoulders.
See if it's possible to sit with no tension in
your body.

HEALING ENERGY

If you can sit in meditation on your own, quietly and peacefully, that is already relaxing and healing. Even if nobody else knows you are meditating, the energy you produce is very beneficial for you and for the world. But if you sit with others, if you walk and work with others, the energy is amplified, and you will create a powerful collective energy of mindfulness for your own healing and the healing of the world. It's something one person cannot do alone. Don't deprive the world of this essential spiritual food.

COLLECTIVE ENERGY
OF HEALING

Usually we think of relaxing and healing as things that happen when we are
alone. But many thousands of people have
participated in collective walking meditation and mass sitting meditation in some
of the world's busiest cities. People have
walked mindfully and peacefully around
the Hoan Kiem Lake in Hanoi. They have
left footprints of peace and freedom on
the ancient streets and piazzas of Rome.
Thousands of us have sat in silence and
stillness in London's busy Trafalgar Square
and in Zucotti Park in New York City.
Everyone who participates and everyone
who witnesses this collective practice has
a chance to get in touch with the energy
of peace, freedom, healing, and joy. The

collective energy generated on such occasions is a gift that we can offer ourselves, one another, the city, and the world.

CULTIVATING JOY

We may think of joy as something that happens spontaneously. But joy needs to be cultivated and practiced in order to grow. When we sit in mindfulness with others, it's easier to sit. When we relax with others, it's easier to relax. The collective energy can help us when we're tired or when our mind wanders. The collective energy can bring us back to ourselves. This is why it's so important to practice with others. At first we may worry that we aren't doing sitting or walking meditation properly, and we may hesitate to practice with others for fear of being judged. But we all know how to sit and how to breathe. That's all we have to do. After only a few moments of concentrating on our breathing, we can bring peace and calm to our body and mind. We only need to pay attention to our in-breath and out-breath. Just focus on that. That's all it takes to begin to calm the agitation in your mind and body and restore stability and peace within yourself. The concentration of those around you will also support you as you begin to practice. Do this a little bit each day, alone or with others. When you train like this, it becomes easier and easier to return to your mindful breathing. The more you train yourself, the more easily you touch the depths of your consciousness, and the more easily you can generate the energy of compassion. Each one of us can do this.

PRACTICING JOY TOGETHER

We can't try hard to relax, just as we can't use a lot of strict effort to be mindful. When we practice together as a community, our practice of mindfulness becomes more joyful, more relaxed, and steady. We are bells of mindfulness for each other, supporting and reminding each other along the path of practice. With the support of the community, we can cultivate peace and joy in ourselves, which we can then offer to those around us. We cultivate our solidity and freedom, our understanding and compassion. We practice looking deeply to gain the sort of insight that can free us from suffering, fear, discrimination, and misunderstanding.

MINDFULNESS OF THE BODY

In our body there may be tension and pain.
If we suppress or ignore this, then every
day the tension and pain will grow and
prevent us from experiencing the happiness that we should be able to experience.
When we have tension in our body, we
can't sleep well or eat well. Mindfulness
of breathing can help us relax and bring
peace to our body. We take care of
our body first. We can take care of our
mind later.

COMMUNICATING WITH OURSELVES

Sometimes we want to relax because we want to not think. That's wonderful; we all need non-thinking time. But that doesn't mean we should stop listening. When we stop thinking, we can start communicating with ourselves by listening to our bodies and our emotions. With all the technology we have, we need only a few seconds to get in contact with people who live very far away. But true communication with others can't happen unless we stop, relax, and listen to ourselves.

RESTORING WELLNESS

Releasing any tension and bringing calm
to your body is the first step in restoring
wellness. You can't heal your body if you
don't pay attention to it. Bringing your
mind home to your body, you become
established in the here and the now.
You have a chance to be aware, without
judgment, of any pain, tension, or suffering
in your body. This is the beginning
of healing.

PEACEFUL BREATHING

When we begin practicing awareness of
our breath, the breathing may not be very
peaceful. It may be rushed, uneven, or
shallow. This is because of the tensions
in our body and the sadness and other
preoccupations in our mind. Therefore, our
breathing isn't peaceful. Breathing in and
out, we concentrate just on our breathing.
If we continue to practice awareness of
breathing, our breathing becomes gentle,
deeper, more peaceful, and the state of
dispersion in our mind ceases. Here are
three exercises to bring peace to the breath.
The first is to recognize the in-breath as
an in-breath, and the out-breath as an
out-breath. The second is to recognize the
length of the in-breath and out-breath.

The third is to focus on the breath all the way through. This is concentration. We just observe the breath; we never force it. We allow it to be natural. With awareness of breathing, our breath naturally becomes deeper, slower, and more peaceful.

Breathing in, I know I'm breathing in.
Breathing out, I know I'm breathing out.

Breathing in, I see my breath is long or short.
Breathing out, I see my breath is long or short.

Breathing in, I follow my in-breath
all the way through.
Breathing out, I follow my out-breath
all the way through.

THE SOUND OF THE BELL

I started inviting the bell when I was sixteen years old, the age when I became
a novice monk. We say, "invite the bell"
rather than "strike the bell" because we
think of the bell as a friend. We want to
invite its sound into our bodies. Inviting
a bell to sound is one very simple way to
relax. When we hear the bell, we breathe
in and we breathe out, and we take in that
beautiful sound. That's it. If we don't have
a bell, we can use another sound—a phone
ringing, an airplane passing overhead, the
chime of a clock, a timer on the computer,
or the natural sounds around us. We can
even use the sound of a jackhammer or a
leaf blower.

BREATHING ROOM

Do you have a space dedicated to relaxing in your home? This doesn't have to be a big space. It could be a small corner (not your bed!) or anywhere in a room that is dedicated just to breathing and relaxing. This is not a space for eating or doing homework, or folding laundry or building anything. This is as essential as a place to eat, sleep, and go to the bathroom. We need a small space where we can take care of our nervous system and restore our tranquility and peace.

BRINGING PEACE TO
OUR TERRITORY

Each of us has a physical body, as well
as feelings, perceptions, thoughts, emotions, and a deep consciousness. These
comprise our territory; and each of us is
a monarch ruling over our territory. But
we're not responsible monarchs. There's
disharmony and conflict in our territory.
We don't have the capacity to restore
peace and harmony. Instead of surveying
our territory, we escape and take refuge
in some form of consumption. Mindfulness
is a practice to give you the courage and
energy to go back and embrace your body
and your feelings and emotions, even if
they're unpleasant. Even if it seems they
may destroy you, go back and embrace
them and help them to transform. If you're

still afraid, ask friends in the practice for support. Practicing walking meditation, conscious breathing, and eating meals in mindfulness, you cultivate the energy of mindfulness and you're able to reign peacefully over your territory.

LAZY DAY

Most of us have very scheduled lives and very full calendars. But do we have enough lazy days in our calendar? A lazy day is a day for us to be without any scheduled activities. We just let the day unfold naturally, timelessly. On this day we have a chance to reestablish the balance in ourselves. We may do walking meditation on our own or with a friend, or do sitting meditation in the forest. We might like to read a little or write home to our family or to a friend. It can be a day for us to look more deeply at our practice and at our relations with others. Or we may recognize that we simply need to rest. When we have unscheduled time, we tend to get bored, seek entertainment, or cast about for something to do. A lazy day is a chance to train ourselves not to be afraid of doing nothing. You might think that not doing anything is a waste of time. But that's not true. Your time is first of all for you to be—to be alive, to be peace.

BEING PEACE

The world needs joyous and loving people who are capable of just being. If you know the art of being peace, then you have the basis for your every action. The ground for action is to be, and the quality of being determines the quality of doing. Action must be based on non-action. People sometimes say, "Don't just sit there, do something." But we have to reverse that statement to say, "Don't just do something, sit there," in order to be in such a way that peace, understanding, and compassion are possible.

RELAXATION NEEDS INSIGHT

We know that there are those who try very hard to be mindful, and yet they cannot relax. They try to breathe and they try to walk; they try very hard, and yet they're unable to relax—because trying is not mindfulness. It's not because you have the intention to relax that you can relax. It's not because you have the intention to stop that you can stop. Mindfulness, true mindfulness, must carry within it true view, insight. You need insight in order to relax.

MINDFULNESS OF SOMETHING

Mindfulness is always mindfulness *of* something. We can be mindful of our breath, our footsteps, our thoughts, and our actions. Mindfulness requires that we bring all our attention to whatever we're doing, whether we're walking, breathing, brushing our teeth, or eating a snack. To be mindful is already to be awakened. If we can say with awareness, "Breathing in, I know I have a body," that is already insight. Because if we know we have a body, we can know how to take care of our body. If we want to reduce stress and tension, we need to be aware that we've been running a lot. True happiness isn't found in success, money, fame, or power. True happiness should be found in the here and the now. With that kind of insight you can truly relax.

RELAXING IN NATURE

When you walk in the hills, in a park, or along a riverbank, you can follow your breathing. When you feel tired or irritated, you can lie down with your arms at your sides, allowing all your muscles to relax, maintaining awareness of just your breath and your smile. Relaxing in this way is wonderful, and quite refreshing. You'll benefit a lot if you practice this several times a day. Your mindful breath and your smile will bring happiness to you and to those around you. There's nothing you could buy your loved ones that could give them as much true happiness as your gift of awareness, breathing, and smiling—and these precious gifts cost nothing.

HEALING OURSELVES, HEALING THE EARTH

Mindfulness and a deep awareness of the Earth can help us to handle pain and difficult feelings. It can help us heal our own suffering and increase our capacity to be aware of the suffering of others. With awareness of the Earth's generosity, we can generate a pleasant feeling. Knowing how to create moments of joy and happiness is crucial for our healing. It's important to be able to see the wonders of life around us and to recognize all the conditions for happiness that already exist. Then, with the energy of mindfulness, we can recognize and embrace our feelings of anger, fear, and despair and transform them. We don't need to become overwhelmed by these unpleasant emotions.

WAKING UP TO THE MOMENT

Walking meditation is a way of waking up to the wonderful moment we are living in. If our mind is caught, preoccupied with our worries and our suffering, or if we distract ourselves with other things while walking, we can't practice mindfulness; we can't enjoy the present moment. We're missing out on life. But if we're awake, then we'll see this is a wonderful moment that life has given us, the only moment in which life is available. We can value each step we take, and each step can bring us happiness because we're in touch with life, with the source of happiness, and with our beloved planet.

TRANSFORMING AN UNPLEASANT SOUND

One day during a retreat in the mountains of northern California there was a wildfire nearby. All day long, during sitting meditation, walking meditation, and silent meals we heard the sound of helicopters. In Vietnam during the war, the sound of helicopters meant guns, bombs, and death. At the retreat there were many practitioners of Vietnamese origin who had gone through the war, so the sound was not pleasant for them, nor was it pleasant for the other practitioners. But there was no choice. So we chose to practice listening to the sound of the helicopters with mindfulness. With mindfulness, we could tell ourselves that this is not a helicopter operating in a situation of war, but a helicopter that is helping to extinguish the flames. With mindfulness, we transform our unpleasant feeling into a pleasant feeling of gratefulness. So we practiced breathing in and out with the sound of helicopters. And we survived very well. We made the sound of helicopters into something helpful. And we practiced:

I listen, I listen.
This sound of helicopters
brings me back
to the present moment.

SLEEPING

When you're in bed and unable to sleep, the best thing to do is to go back to your breathing. Resting is almost as beneficial as sleeping, and you'll know you're doing the best that you can. Bring peace to your breathing and your body so you can rest.

LEARNING TO REST

We have to relearn the art of resting. Even when we have a vacation, we don't know how to make use of it. Very often we are more tired after a vacation than before it. We should learn the art of relaxation and resting, and make some time each day to practice deep relaxation on our own or with others.

LEANING ON SNORING

Sometimes you have to share a room with someone who snores. You may get irritated. But with mindfulness you can bring about compassion. You can lean on the sound of snoring in order to go to sleep. Listen and say that this brings you home to the here and now. Then you can accept the snoring much more easily, and you can go to sleep thanks to the sound of snoring.

OUR IDEA OF HAPPINESS

Say you have a notion of happiness, an
idea about what will make you happy.
That idea has its roots in you and in your
environment. Your idea tells you what
conditions you need in order to be happy.
You've entertained this idea for ten or
twenty years, and now you realize that
your idea of happiness is making you
suffer. Your idea may contain an element
of delusion, anger, or craving. These
elements are the substance of suffering.
On the other hand, you know that you have
other kinds of experiences: moments of
joy, release, or true love. You can recognize
these as moments of real happiness. When
you've had a moment of real happiness, it
becomes easier to release the objects of

your craving, because you're developing the insight that these objects will not make you happy.

Many people have the desire to let go, but they're not able to do so because they don't yet have enough insight; they haven't seen other alternatives, other doorways to peace and happiness. Fear is an element that prevents us from letting go. We're fearful that if we let go we'll have nothing else to cling to. Letting go is a practice; it's an art. One day, when you're strong enough and determined enough, you'll let go of the afflictions that make you suffer.

LETTING GO

To "let go" means to let go of *something*. That something may be an object of our mind, something we've created, like an idea, feeling, desire, or belief. Getting stuck on that idea could bring a lot of unhappiness and anxiety. We'd like to let it go, but how? It's not enough just to want to let it go; we have to recognize it first as being something real. We have to look deeply into its nature and where it has come from, because ideas are born from feelings, emotions, and past experiences, from things we've seen and heard. With the energy of mindfulness and concentration we can look deeply and discover the roots of the idea, feeling, emotion, or desire. Mindfulness and concentration bring about insight, and insight can help us release the object in our mind.

SOLITUDE

Being in solitude can help us relax. Solitude doesn't mean being by ourselves or away from civilization. Real solitude means we're not carried away by the crowd, by sorrows about the past, by worries about the future, or by strong emotions in the present. We don't lose our stability and our peace. We take refuge in our mindful breathing and come back to the present moment, and to the island of peace within ourselves. We enjoy our time with others, but we don't get lost in our interactions. Even in a busy marketplace, we can smile and breathe in peace, dwelling in the island of ourselves.

LETTING GO OF WORRYING

Our practice is to learn to take care of the present moment. Don't allow yourself to be lost in the past or the future. Taking good care of the present moment, we may be able to change the negative things from the past and prepare for a good future. We tend to worry about what will happen in the future. The practice helps us to come home to the present moment, to our body, our feelings, to the environment around us. When we breathe in and breathe out mindfully, our mind is brought back to our body, and we are truly there in order to take care of the present moment. If there's some stress, some tension in our body, we practice mindful breathing in order to release the tension, and that brings us relief. If there's a painful feeling in us, we use mindfulness to embrace our feeling so that we can get relief. The key point is that you are fully there in the present moment, in the here and now, to take care of yourself and what's happening around you. You don't think too much about the future or project too much about how it might be; and you're not trapped too much in the past. You have to train yourself, to learn how to go home to the present moment, to the here and now, and to take care of that moment, to take care of your body and your feelings in this moment. As you learn how to be in the present moment, you'll gain faith and trust in your ability to handle the situation. You learn how to take care of your feelings and what's happening around you. That makes you confident; and as your confidence grows, you're no longer the victim of your worries.

HAPPINESS IS A
COLLECTIVE MATTER

We can learn to handle our own fear and
pain. After that, we can help other people, because we have direct experience
with how to handle the fear and the pain.
Suffering and fear are not things that we
just experience by ourselves. Our fear and
suffering is also the suffering of our parents,
our friends, and our society. You are me and
I am you. If something wonderful happens
to one of us, it happens to all of us. If something awful happens to one of us, it happens
to all of us. This answer comes from the
insight of no-self. With the insight of no-self
you see that your suffering, your fear, is a
collective suffering. With the insight of no-
self, you see that happiness is a collective
happiness. We are not separated.

WALKING YOUR TALK

If you practice mindfulness to release the tension, stress, and pain in your body, you begin to feel better. Then, when you see a person who is tense, who has pain in his or her body, you can show him or her how to practice. That person will believe you because you have direct experience. You've walked your talk. That's why it's very important that we're able to do it for ourselves first. Just the way you live your life, the way you react to situations, can already be very helpful. Other people see you react in a peaceful and kind way, and they already begin to learn from you.

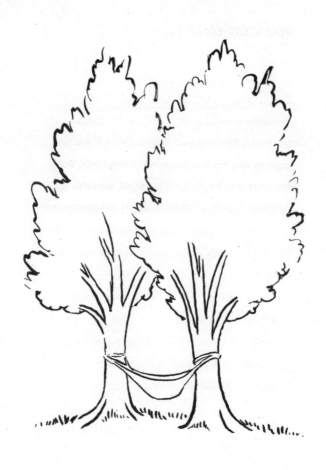

EFFORTLESSNESS

Do we need to make a special effort to see the beauty of the blue sky? Do we have to practice to be able to enjoy it? No, we just enjoy it. Each second, each minute of our lives can be like this. Wherever we are, at any time, we have the capacity to enjoy the sunshine, the presence of each other, even the sensation of our breathing. We don't need to go to China to enjoy the blue sky. We don't have to travel into the future to enjoy our breathing. We can be in touch with these things right now. It would be a pity if we were only aware of suffering.

LETTING GO OF STRESS

Stress accumulates in our body. The way we eat, drink, and live takes its toll on our well-being. Lying down and bringing gentle awareness to our breath, we can realize rest and recovery for our physical body. Find space in your day when you can practice mindful breathing and letting go of tensions. In just five, ten, or twenty minutes, you can reestablish mindfulness and dissipate stress. When you have trouble sleeping, follow your breathing in and breathing out. Bring your awareness to the different parts of your body in turn, and allow them to relax. Sometimes this can help you get to sleep. The practice is still very good even if you don't sleep, because it nourishes you and allows you to rest.

LIFE IS DREADFUL
AND WONDERFUL

Meditation means being aware of what is going on—in our bodies, in our feelings, in our minds, and in the world. Each day thousands of children die of hunger. Plant and animal species are going extinct every day. Yet the sunrise is beautiful, and the rose that bloomed this morning along the wall is a miracle. Life is both dreadful and wonderful. To practice meditation is to be in touch with both aspects of life.

DON'T WASTE YOUR LIFE

On the wooden board outside of the meditation hall in many Zen monasteries, there is a four-line inscription. The last line is, "Do not squander your life." Our lives are made of days and hours, and each hour is precious. Have we wasted our hours and our days? Are we wasting our lives? When we practice sitting or walking meditation, it's easier to be mindful and concentrated. During the rest of the day, we also practice. It's more difficult, but it's possible. The sitting and the walking can be extended to the non-walking, non-sitting moments of our day. That is the basic principle of meditation.

HAPPINESS AND AWARENESS

Please do not think we must be solemn in order to meditate. Whether or not we are happy depends on our awareness. When you have a toothache, you think that not having a toothache will make you very happy. But when you don't have a tooth-ache, often you are still not happy. All of us have the capacity of transforming neutral feelings into pleasant feelings. If you're rested and relaxed, all living beings will profit from your relaxation and energy. This is the most basic kind of peace work.

SMILING

A smile can relax hundreds of muscles in
your face, and relax your nervous system.
A smile makes you master of yourself.
All day long, we can practice smiling.
At first you may find it difficult to smile,
and we have to think about why. Smiling
means that we are ourselves, that we have
sovereignty over ourselves, that we are not
drowned in forgetfulness. I'd like to offer
a short poem you can recite from time to
time, while breathing and smiling:

Breathing in, I calm my body.
Breathing out, I smile.
Dwelling in the present moment,
I know this is a wonderful moment.

CALMING

"Breathing in, I calm my body." Reciting this line is like drinking a glass of cool water—you feel the freshness permeate your body. When I breathe in and recite this line, I actually feel the breathing calming my body, calming my mind.

PRESENT MOMENT, WONDERFUL MOMENT

While I sit here, I don't long to be somewhere else; I'm not pulled away by the
future or by the past. I sit here, and I know
where I am. This is very important. We
tend to be alive in the future, not now. We
say, "Wait until I finish school and get my
PhD; then I'll really be living." Once we
have it—and it wasn't easy to get—we say
to ourselves, "I have to wait until I have a
job for my life to really begin." Then after
the job a car, and after the car a house. We
aren't capable of being alive in the present moment. We tend to postpone being
alive to the future, the distant future, we
don't know when. It's as if now is not the
moment to be alive. We may never be alive
at all in our entire life. The only moment to
be alive is in the present moment.

SELF-HEALING

We have to believe in our body's capacity
to heal itself. The power of self-healing is
a reality, but many of us don't believe in it.
Instead, we take a lot of vitamins and medi-
cines that may sometimes be harmful to
our body. Taking good care of our bodies,
eating well but not too much, sleeping, and
drinking water, we have to trust the power
of understanding, healing, and loving within
us. It is our refuge. If we lose our faith
and confidence in it, we lose everything.
Instead of panicking or giving ourselves
up to despair, we practice mindful breathing and put our trust in the healing power
within us. We call this the island within ourselves in which we can take refuge. It is an
island of peace, confidence, solidity, love,

and freedom. Be that island for yourself.
You don't have to look elsewhere. Mindful
breathing helps you go back to that precious
island within, so that you can experience
the foundation of your being.

THE WAR INSIDE

We know that many of us don't want to go home to ourselves. We're afraid. There's a lot of internal suffering and conflict that we want to avoid. We complain that we don't have time to live, yet we try to kill our free time by not going back to ourselves. We escape by turning on the television or picking up a novel or a magazine; or we go out for a drive. We run away from ourselves and don't attend to our body, feelings, or states of mind. We have to go home. If we're at war with our parents, friends, society, or our church, it may be because there's a war raging within us. An internal war facilitates other wars. We're afraid of going home because we lack the tools or the means for self-protection. Equipped with mindfulness, we can go home safely and not be overwhelmed by our pain, sorrow, and depression. With some training, with the practice of mindful walking and mindful breathing, we'll be able to go home and embrace our pain and sorrow.

WATER OVER THE ROCKS

The activities of our mind, often unstable and agitated, are like a torrent of water washing over the rocks. In traditional Buddhist literature, the mind is often compared to a monkey always swinging from branch to branch or to a horse galloping out of control. Once our mind is able to identify what is happening, we will be able to see clearly our mental state and make it calm. Just that will bring us peace, joy, and stillness.

BOAT IN A STORM

Suppose you're on a boat crossing the ocean. If you get caught in a storm, it's important to stay calm and not panic. To accomplish that, go back to your breathing and be yourself. When you're calm, truly your own island, you will know what to do and what not to do. Otherwise, the boat may capsize. We destroy ourselves by doing things we ought not to do. Take refuge in mindfulness, and you will see things more clearly and know how to improve the situation. Mindfulness brings about concentration, and concentration brings about insight and wisdom. This is the safest refuge. The safety and stability your island can provide depend on your practice. Everything—comforting a child, building a house, or playing volleyball—depends on your practice.

ALL IS NOT SUFFERING

There are those who say that everything is suffering. This is not true. It's an exaggeration and a misunderstanding of what the Buddha said. The Buddha said that there is suffering, but he didn't say that's all there is. There are causes that bring about suffering, and it's possible to arrive at a state of the absence of these causes. Of course we shouldn't dream that one day we'll have one hundred percent happiness and not a single drop of suffering. There is always something. But we can handle suffering and happiness in an artful way.

RELEASING TENSION

The way to release all the tension is with our mindful breath. So we always start with mindfulness. Mindfulness brings the mind to the present moment, and we see and experience things more deeply. Going back to the present moment, you can see if your body is tense. We look deeply and see that, "Ah, I am tense because I'm carried away by my worry, anxiety, and plans." Then we can make the determination not to be carried away like that.

DESIRE AND HAPPINESS

The Buddha often said that many people confuse desire with happiness. Before he became a monk, the Buddha had grown up as a prince and had tasted a life of trying to satisfy desires, so his words came from experience. He said that true happiness is a life with few desires, few possessions, and the time to enjoy the many wonders in us and around us. Desire means to be caught in unwholesome longing. When the mind is desiring, we are aware of the presence of that state of mind. "This is the mind longing for wealth." "This is the mind desiring reputation." When the mind isn't desiring, it's important to observe that the desiring mind is not present. "This is the sense of ease that accompanies the absence of a mind desiring wealth." "This is the sense of ease that accompanies the absence of a mind desiring reputation," etc. We can experience happiness, ease, and peace when we observe these moments of no desire. Desirelessness is the basic condition that makes possible the feelings of joy, peace, and ease that come with living a simple life. Simplicity means to have few desires, to be content with a simple life and just a few possessions. Desirelessness is the basis of true happiness, because in true happiness there must be the elements of peace, joy, and ease.

RELAXING WHERE WE ARE

Living in the city, we may be very busy, and the city is very noisy and polluted. We can never see the moon or the stars, and we get caught in the city. We want to have a two-day vacation to leave the city and go to the countryside, but we can't go because we're not able to let go. One day a friend comes and says, "This Friday let's go to the countryside." That person is really good at convincing us to leave, so we accept. We get in the car, and after only forty-five minutes we have left the city behind and we can see the countryside. We feel the breeze, we see the spaciousness, and it gives us joy. That joy comes from being able to let go and leave the city behind. Letting go gives rise to joy and happiness. We need to sit down with a piece of paper and write down the things we can let go of. We're still caught in many things. We're not happy and joyful, because we haven't been able to let go.

IDEAS OF HAPPINESS

In order to be happy, we need first of all
to let go of our ideas of happiness. It's
difficult. Each one of us has an idea of
happiness; we think that we must have
this or that to be happy, or that we have to
eliminate this or that to be happy. We think
that we have to have certain conditions:
We have to have this house or this car or
that person to live with us so that we can
be happy. We have these ideas of happiness. If we haven't been able to be happy
and joyful, it's because we're caught in
our ideas. So we have to be able to let
them go. Our idea of happiness is the main
obstacle to happiness.

NO COWS TO LOSE

One day the Buddha was sitting having a silent lunch together with his monks in the woods. A farmer came hurrying by and asked, "Dear monks, have you seen my cows? They have all left me this morning. If I don't have my cows, how can I live? Insects have eaten my fields of sesame; I couldn't harvest anything. I cannot live. I think I will kill myself." The Buddha said, "Dear friend, we've been sitting here for a while, and we haven't seen any cows pass by. Maybe you can look in another direction." So the farmer left. The Buddha turned to his monks and said, "Dear monks, you are very lucky. You don't have any cows to lose." A cow stands for something we need to let go of. Our idea of happiness is a cow. And it's because of this idea of happiness that we cannot be happy.

NAMING OUR COWS

Each one of us needs to sit down with a piece of paper and write down the names of all our cows. Among them are our ideas of happiness. We get caught and we suffer. We struggle with all these things, but we don't have the capacity to let them go. How many cows do we have? Sometimes we see that one page is not enough for us to write the names of all our cows. The truth is, if you let go of these cows, you will be lighter, and your happiness will be much greater. Let go so that happiness, joy, and peace can be possible.

OUR PEACE IS WHAT IS MOST PRECIOUS

Awakening is something that happens today, not in ten or twenty years. Insights can come continuously to give us the understanding we need to untangle ourselves from attachments. When our mind is entangled with anger, jealousy, or sadness, we can be in that state hour after hour, day after day. It's a pity, because meanwhile, life is wondrous. If we only concentrate on breathing in and seeing that our body is a wonder, we can see that nothing else is really important. It's only the peace in our body and in our mind that matters. Anyone can attain this insight. While we sit, we can be with our breathing, we can let go of tensions, and we can have peace. This peace is the most precious thing there is, more precious than any pursuit.

FREEDOM IS A PRACTICE

If you want to be free, just concentrate on your in-breath and out-breath. Breathe in and out for three minutes, and in those three minutes you are free. This freedom is something we have to train ourselves to have. It's not something that comes automatically. When we have freedom, when we're not overwhelmed by anger or anxiety, then we can make the determination to practice cultivating this freedom. When we're anxious, worried, or angry, we can't make good decisions. When we're free, we make better decisions. This freedom is something we can attain whenever we like with the practice of breathing in mindfulness, walking in mindfulness.

DON'T BE TOO BUSY

As you go about your daily activities, do you feel you're lacking something? As you wash the dishes, cook a meal, clean the kitchen, while you walk, stand, sit, or lie down, what are you looking for? There's no business for you to take care of. You're free; there's nothing to do or to run after. Perhaps you're seeking something, calculating, or feeling agitated. Your feet and hands may always think they have to be doing something. When you do sitting or walking meditation, don't put too much effort into it. You're not trying to attain something. Meditation shouldn't be hard labor. The principle is to be ordinary, not to be too busy. We just live in a normal way. When we eat, we just eat; we don't speak. If we need to urinate, we urinate. If we're tired, then we can rest.

COMPASSION FOR YOURSELF

Don't consider anger, hatred, and greed
as enemies you have to fight, destroy,
or annihilate. If you annihilate anger, you
annihilate yourself. Dealing with anger
in that way would be like transforming
yourself into a battlefield, and tearing
yourself to bits. If you struggle in that
way, you do violence to yourself. If you
can't be compassionate to yourself, you
won't be able to be compassionate to
others. When we get angry, we have to
produce awareness: "I am angry. Anger is in
me. I am anger." That is the first thing to do.

Breathing in, I feel my anger.
Breathing out, I smile.
I stay with my breathing
so I won't lose myself.

NO BLAMING

When you plant a tree, if it doesn't grow well, you don't blame the tree. You look into the reasons it isn't doing well. It may need fertilizer or more water or less sun. We never blame the tree. Yet we're quick to blame our child. If we know how to take care of her, she will grow well, like a tree. Blaming has no good effect at all. Never blame, never try to persuade using reason and arguments; they never lead to any positive effect. That is my experience. No argument, no reasoning, no blaming, just understanding. If you understand, and you show that you understand, you can love, and the situation will change.

THE BREATH IS A BRIDGE

Our breath is like a bridge connecting body and mind. In our daily lives, our bodies may be in one place and our minds somewhere else, in the past, or in the future. This is called a state of distraction. The breath is a connection between the body and the mind. When you begin to breathe in and out mindfully, your mind will come back to your body. You will be able to realize the oneness of body and mind and become fully present and fully alive in the here and the now. You will be in a position to touch life deeply in this moment. This isn't something difficult. Everyone can do it.

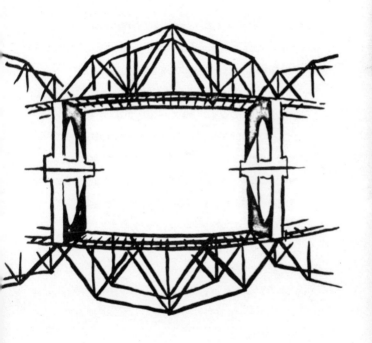

RELAXED PRACTICE

In traditional Chinese medicine, doctors sometimes offer their patients something healing that is delicious to eat. Just by eating, you begin to heal in a pleasant and relaxed way. The same is true with the practice. While you practice sitting, you enjoy sitting. While you practice breathing, you enjoy breathing. If you are able to enjoy yourself, then healing and transformation will take place.

LIBERATION

We often live as if we're in a dream. We're
dragged into the past or pulled into the
future. We're bound by our sorrow, agitation, and fear. We hold on to our anger,
which blocks communication. "Liberation"
means transforming and transcending
these conditions in order to be fully awake,
at ease, peaceful, joyful, and fresh. We
practice stopping and observing deeply in
order to arrive at liberation. When we live
in this way, our life is worth living, and we
become a source of joy to our family and
to everyone around us.

RELAXED SITTING

When you sit and watch television, you
don't make any effort. That's why you can
sit there for a long time. When you sit in
meditation, if you struggle, you won't be
able to sit for very long. Please imitate
the way you sit in your living room.
Effortlessness is the key to success. Don't
fight. Don't try hard. Just allow yourself to
sit. This relaxing way of sitting is also restful.
Allow your body to rest and be at ease.

SETTLING DOWN

When you pour fresh juice into a glass and let it stand for fifteen minutes, all the pulp sinks down to the bottom of the glass. If you allow yourself to sit in a relaxed, peaceful way, it calms and settles your body and your mind. Sitting like this allows you to enjoy your in-breath and out-breath, to enjoy being alive, to enjoy just sitting there.

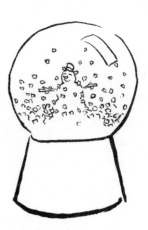

THE HABIT OF TENSION

A number of years ago, I went to India to visit the Buddhist community of untouchables. A friend had organized the teaching tour for me. He belonged to that caste, which has been discriminated against for so many thousands of years. He was sitting next to me in the bus, on my right. I was enjoying looking out the window and seeing the countryside of India. But when I looked at him, I saw that he was very tense. He had done everything to make my visit pleasant, yet he continued to worry. This habit energy had been transmitted to him from many generations of ancestors who had struggled all their lives against discrimination. It's hard to transform that kind of habit. I said, "Dear friend, why are you so tense? You have arranged everything beautifully. There's nothing to do now that we're here on the bus; and when we arrive, our friends will come to the station to meet us. Sit back and relax and enjoy the countryside." He said, "Okay," but just two minutes later, he looked exactly as before, very tense, worrying about the future, and not being able to be at ease in the here and now. So many of us are like that. Our practice is to stop running, and to be aware that all the wonders of life are available in the here and now.

MEDITATIONS
FOR RESTING
AND RELAXING

INVITING THE BELL

There is tranquility, peace, and joy within us, but we have to call them forth so they can manifest. Inviting a bell to sound is one way to call forth the joy and tranquility within. I have been inviting the bell since I was sixteen. When I want to invite the small bell, I hold it in the palm of my hand and I breathe in and out. "Breathing in, I calm myself. Breathing out, I smile." If you want to invite the bell, here is a short poem to learn by heart. Recite the first line of the poem as you breathe in, the second line as you breathe out, and so on:

Body, speech, and mind in perfect oneness,
I send my heart along with the sound of this bell.
May all the hearers awaken from forgetfulness,
and transcend the path of anxiety and sorrow.

LISTENING TO THE BELL

The bell is a friend, someone who helps us come back to ourselves and become calm. We invite tranquility to manifest. With the help of the bell, our mind is collected and brought back to the present moment. We stop our thinking and talking and come back to ourselves, breathing and relaxing. As you listen, you may notice that your in-breath and out-breath naturally become longer and more relaxed. Here is a poem for listening to the bell. "Your true home" means your own island, your solidity, peace, and joy.

Listen, listen.
This wonderful sound
brings me back
to my true home.

EASING WORRY

Sometimes we think and worry nonstop.
It's like having a cassette tape continually
turning in our minds. When we leave the
television set on for a long time, it becomes
hot. Our head also gets hot from all our
thinking. When we can't stop, we may
be unable to sleep well. Even if we take
a sleeping pill, we continue to run, think,
and worry in our dreams. The alternative
medicine is mindful breathing. If we practice
mindful breathing for five minutes, allowing
our body to rest, then we stop thinking for
that time. We can use words like "in" and
"out" to help us be aware of our breathing.
This is not thinking; these words aren't
concepts. They're guides for mindfulness
of breathing. When we think too much, the
quality of our being is reduced. Stopping the

thinking, we increase the quality of our being. There's more peace, relaxation, and rest.

IN, OUT. DEEP, SLOW.

Here is a poem to practice any time, but especially when you're angry, worried, or sad. If you know how to practice this poem, you'll feel much better after just one or two minutes.

> In, Out.
> Deep, Slow.
> Calm, Ease.
> Smile, Release.
> **Present Moment, Wonderful Moment.**

"In, Out," means that when I breathe in, I know I'm breathing in, and when I breathe out, I know I'm breathing out. You are one-hundred percent with your in-breath and your out-breath. Don't think of anything else. That's the secret of success.

After you've practiced "In, Out" three, four, or five times, you'll notice that your in-breath naturally becomes deeper, and your out-breath becomes slower. Your breath is calm, and you're more peaceful. That is "Deep, Slow."

"Calm, Ease" means, "Breathing in, I feel calm. Breathing out, I feel at ease." This exercise is wonderful to practice, especially when you're nervous, or angry, or you don't feel peaceful in yourself.

Then you come to "Smile, Release." "Breathing in, I smile." You may feel it's too difficult to smile. But after practicing three or four times, you may feel that you're able to smile. If you can smile, you'll feel a lot better. You may protest, "Why do you want me to smile? It's not natural." Many people ask me that and they protest, "I have no joy in me. I can't force myself to smile; it wouldn't be true." I always say that a smile can be a kind of yoga practice, yoga of the mouth. You just smile, even if you don't feel joy. And after you smile, you'll see you feel differently. Sometimes the mind takes the initiative, and sometimes you have to allow the body to take the initiative.

BODY SCAN

If you only have a few minutes to sit or lie down and relax, you can do a body scan. Beginning at the top of your head and moving down to your toes, you bring mindful awareness to parts of your body. You can bring attention to many or just a few parts of your body. This can be done anytime, anywhere to rest and relieve stress in body and mind.

Breathing in, I am aware of my eyes.
Breathing out, I smile to my eyes.

Having eyes in good condition is a wonderful thing. We need to take care of our eyes and rest them from time to time, especially when we're working.

Breathing in, I am aware of my heart.

Breathing out, I smile to my heart.

You have neglected your heart for a long time. You may cause trouble for your heart by the way you rest, work, eat, and drink. Your heart works day and night for your well-being, but because of your lack of mindfulness, you have not been very helpful to your heart. Once or twice each day, you can pick at least one part of your body to focus on and practice relaxing.

TELEPHONE MEDITATION

When you want to pick up the phone to
call someone, first practice breathing in
and out to calm yourself.

> Words can travel thousands of miles.
> Words can help restore communication
> and build mutual understanding.
> I vow that the conversation I'm going to have
> will bring us closer together,
> and make our friendship bloom like a flower.

When you receive a call, you can also
practice mindful breathing before
answering the phone.

> I listen, I listen.
> The mindfulness bell of the telephone
> brings me back to my true home.

COMPUTER MEDITATION

A bell is a friend, an invention to help us. If you work on a computer, you might get so carried away by your work that you forget you have a body; you forget that you're alive. You even forget to breathe sometimes. So you may like to program your computer so that every quarter of an hour it offers the sound of the bell, enabling you to go back to yourself, to smile, and to breathe in and out before you continue working. Many of us have done that. The sound of a bell reminding you to come back to yourself and enjoy breathing is a wonderful way to take a break.

DEEP RELAXATION

Deep relaxation is an opportunity for your body to rest, heal, and be restored. You bring attention to each part of your body: hair, scalp, brain, ears, neck, shoulders, arms, hands, fingers, lungs, each of the internal organs, the digestive system, pelvis, legs, feet, toes. You send your love and care to every part of your body and every cell.

Lie down on your back with your arms at your sides. Make yourself comfortable. Allow your body to relax. Be aware of the floor beneath you and the contact of your body with the floor. Allow your body to sink into the floor.

Become aware of your breathing, in and out. Be aware of your abdomen rising and falling as you breathe in and out.

Breathing in, bring your awareness to your eyes. Breathing out, allow your eyes to relax. Allow your eyes to sink back into your head. Let go of the tension in all the tiny muscles around your eyes. Your eyes allow you to see a paradise of forms and colors. Allow your eyes to rest. Send love and gratitude to your eyes.

Breathing in, bring your awareness to your mouth. Breathing out, allow your mouth to relax. Release the tension around your mouth. Your lips are the petals of a flower. Let a gentle smile bloom on your lips. Smiling releases the tension in the hundreds of muscles in your face. Feel the tension release in your cheeks, your jaw, and your throat.

Breathing in, bring your awareness to your shoulders. Breathing out, allow your shoulders to relax. Let them sink into the floor. Let all the accumulated tension flow into the floor. You carry so much with your shoulders. Now let your shoulders relax as you care for them.

Breathing in, become aware of your arms. Breathing out, relax your arms. Let your arms sink into the floor. Relax your upper arms, your elbows, your lower arms, your wrists, your hands, and all the tiny muscles in your fingers. Move your fingers a little if you need to, helping the muscles relax.

Breathing in, bring your awareness to your heart. Breathing out, allow your heart to relax. You have neglected your heart for a long time, and you cause your heart stress by the way you work, eat, and manage anxiety and stress. Your heart beats for you night and day. Embrace your heart with mindfulness and tenderness, reconciling and taking care of your heart.

Breathing in, bring your awareness to your legs. Breathing out, allow your legs to relax. Release all the tension in your legs, your thighs, your knees, your calves, your ankles, your feet, your toes, and all the tiny muscles in your toes. You may want to move your toes a little to help them relax. Send your love and care to your toes.

Breathing in, breathing out, your whole body feels as light as a lily floating on the water. You have nowhere to go, nothing to do. You are free as a cloud floating in the sky.

Bring your awareness back to your breathing, to your abdomen rising and falling.

Following your breathing, become aware of your arms and legs. You may want to move them a little and stretch.

When you feel ready, slowly sit up.

When you are ready, slowly stand up.

Also available from Rider.

How to Sit

Thich Nhat Hanh

THICH NHAT HANH

HOW TO
SIT

'THE FATHER OF MINDFULNESS'
IRISH TIMES

Thich Nhat Hanh considers the mechanics of posture and
breathing, and reveals how the simple act of sitting quietly, at
peace with ourselves and our surroundings, can be a powerful
way to strengthen our inner resources.

ISBN 9781846045141

Order direct from www.penguin.co.uk

How to Eat

Thich Nhat Hanh

THICH NHAT HANH

HOW TO
EAT

'THE FATHER OF MINDFULNESS'
IRISH TIMES

Thich Nhat Hanh invites us to eat mindfully, and shows how each mouthful can nourish us on many different levels. Eating joyfully feeds our sense of compassion and understanding, and helps us achieve a healthy weight.

ISBN 9781846045158

Order direct from www.penguin.co.uk

How to Love

Thich Nhat Hanh

THICH NHAT HANH

HOW TO
LOVE

'THE FATHER OF MINDFULNESS'
IRISH TIMES

Thich Nhat Hanh brings his signature clarity, compassion and
humour to the thorny question of how to love. He shows us
how to open our hearts to ourselves and embrace the world.

ISBN 9781846045172

Order direct from www.penguin.co.uk

How to Walk

Thich Nhat Hanh

THICH NHAT HANH

HOW TO
WALK

'THE FATHER OF MINDFULNESS'
IRISH TIMES

The everyday act of walking can be an opportunity to diminish
depression, recapture wonder and encourage gratitude. Here,
Thich Nhat Hanh explains how each of our steps has the
power to increase our concentration, our insight, and our joy in
being alive.

ISBN 9781846045165

Order direct from www.penguin.co.uk